Bee Three Publishing is an imprint of Books By Boxer
Published by
Books By Boxer, Leeds, LS13 4BS UK
Books by Boxer (EU), Dublin D02 P593 IRELAND

MADE IN CHINA
ISBN: 9781915410184

MIX
Paper | Supporting responsible forestry
FSC™ C007683

This book is produced from responsibly sourced paper to ensure forest management

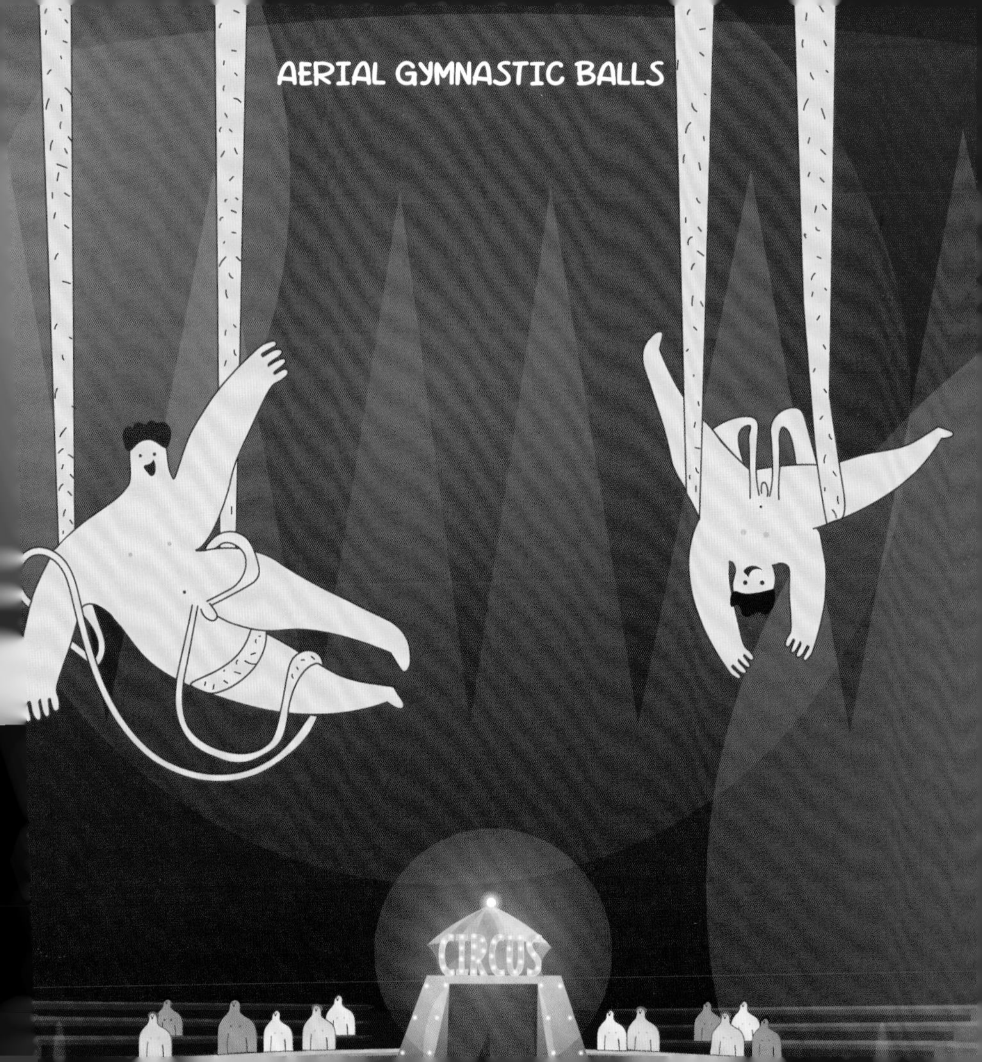
AERIAL GYMNASTIC BALLS
CIRCUS

NEW BELT BALLS

BOW TIE BALLS

ARM WRESTLING BALLS

BASKETBALL BALLS

BIKE HELMET BALLS

BLOCKING HOLE IN THE BOAT BALLS

BOWLING BALLS

BULLFIGHTING BALLS

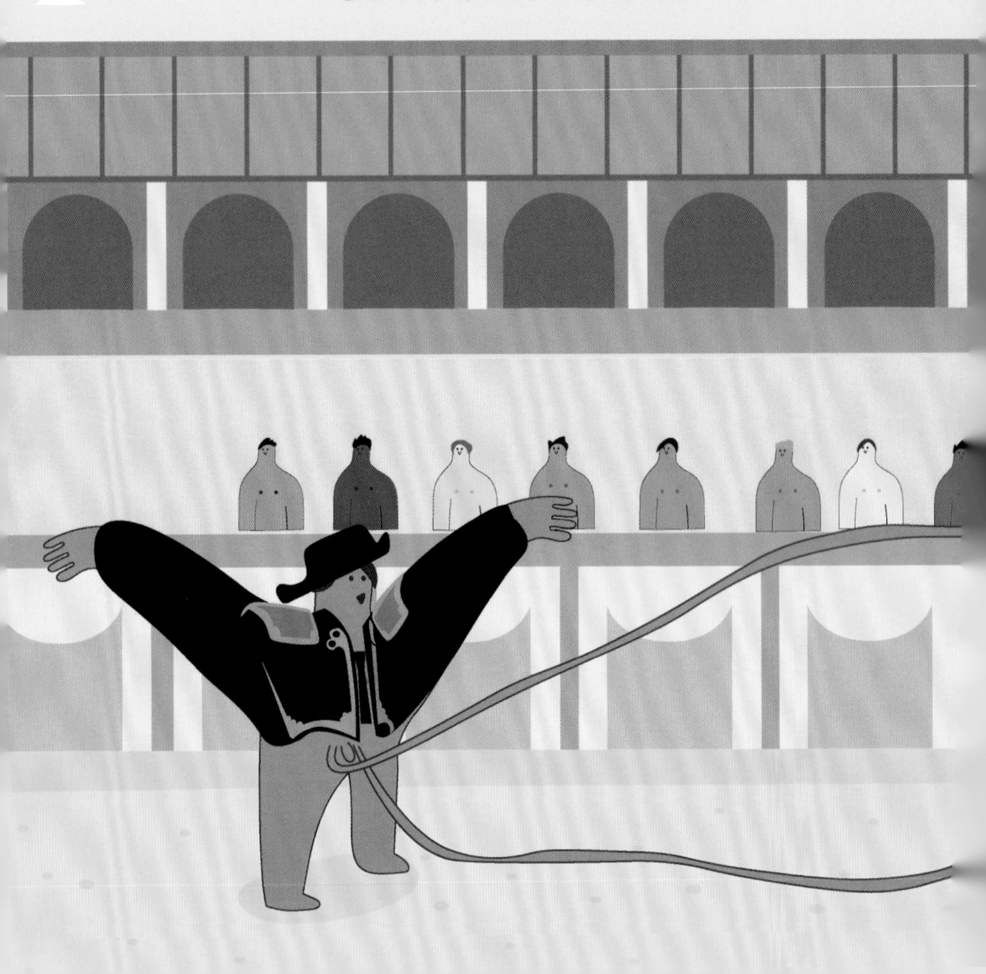

TOBOGGANING BALLS

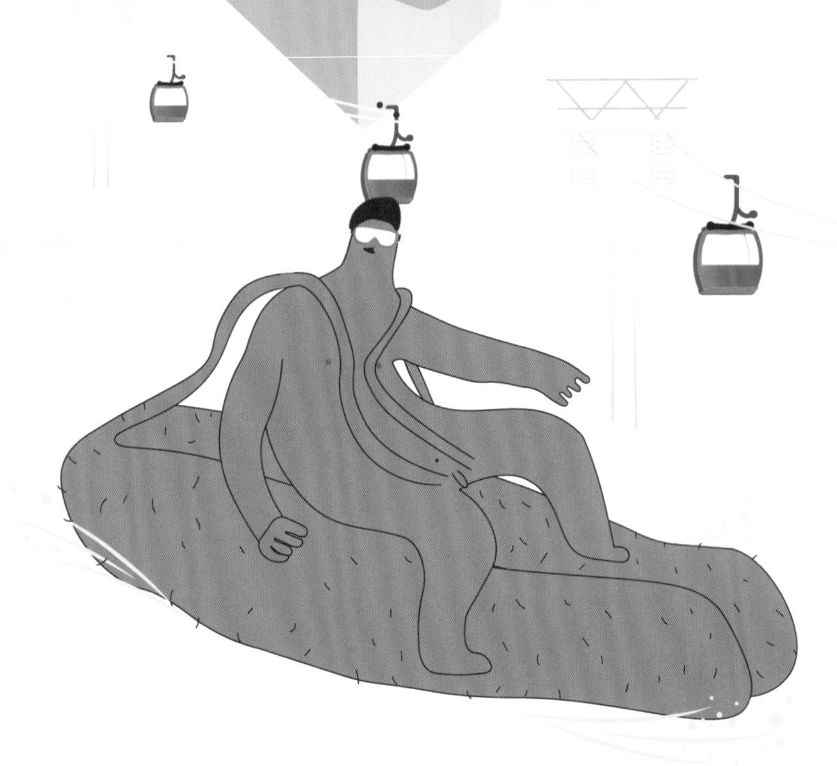

LILO BALLS

BANANA BOAT RIDE BALLS

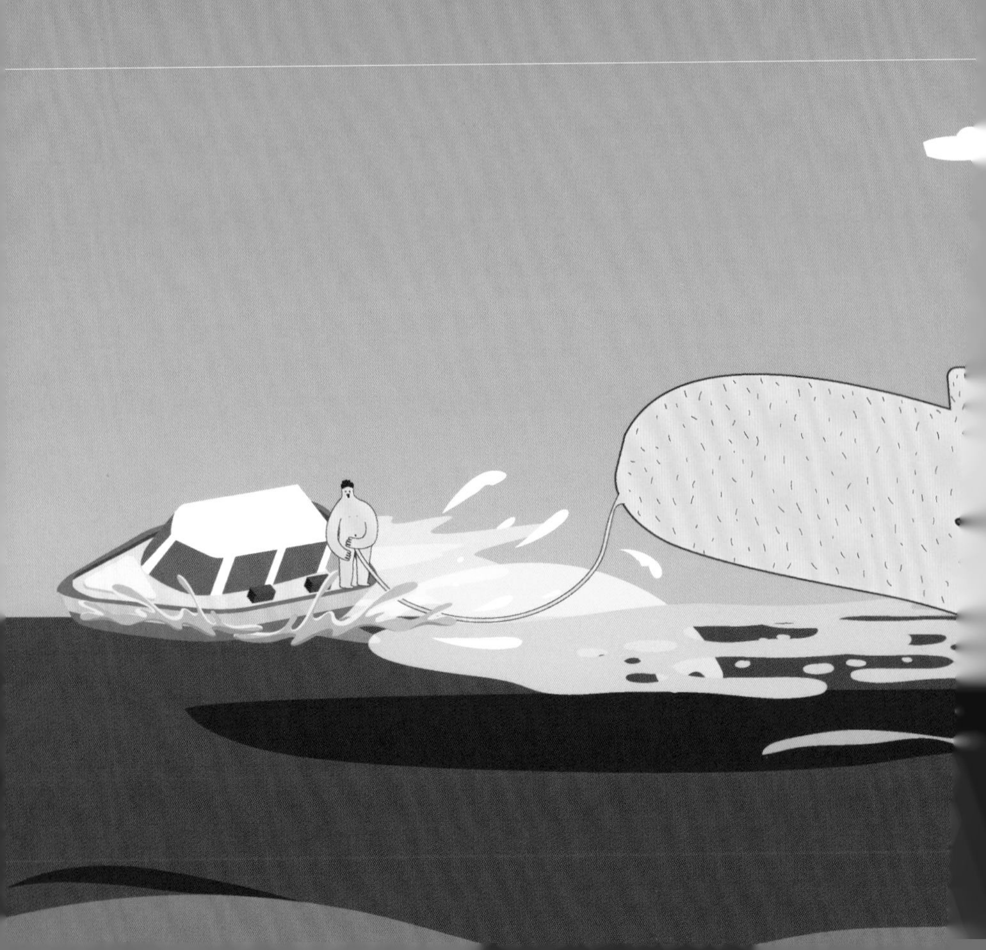

BOOKMARK BALLS

BIKE HORN BALLS

HAPPY BIRTHDAY BALLOON BALLS
21

CAUGHT SHORT BALLS

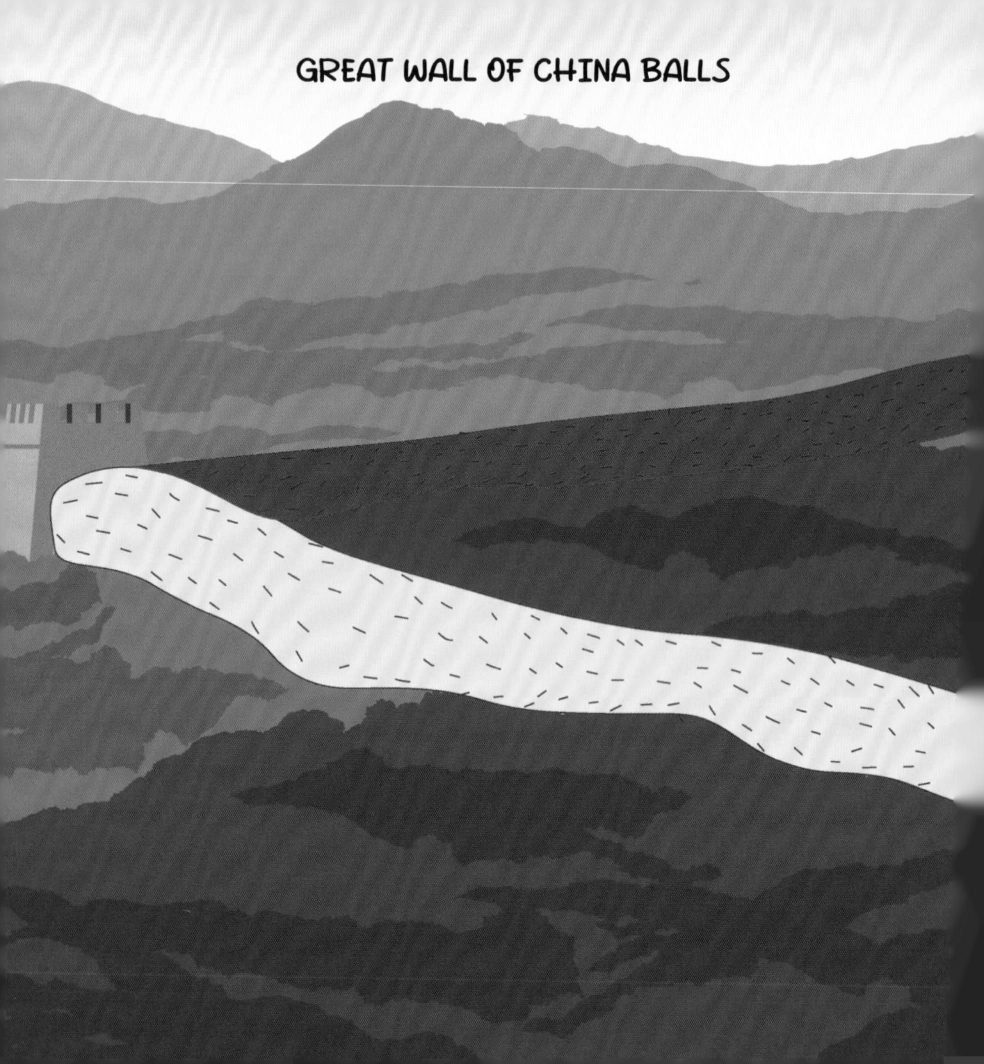
GREAT WALL OF CHINA BALLS

BOUNCY CASTLE BALLS

CAR WASH BALLS

PARCEL DELIVERY BALLS

DISCO BALLS

TEACHING BALLS
ENGLISH VERBS
SPEAK-SPOKE-SPOKEN
RUN-RAN-RUN
READ-READ- READ
GO-WENT-GONE

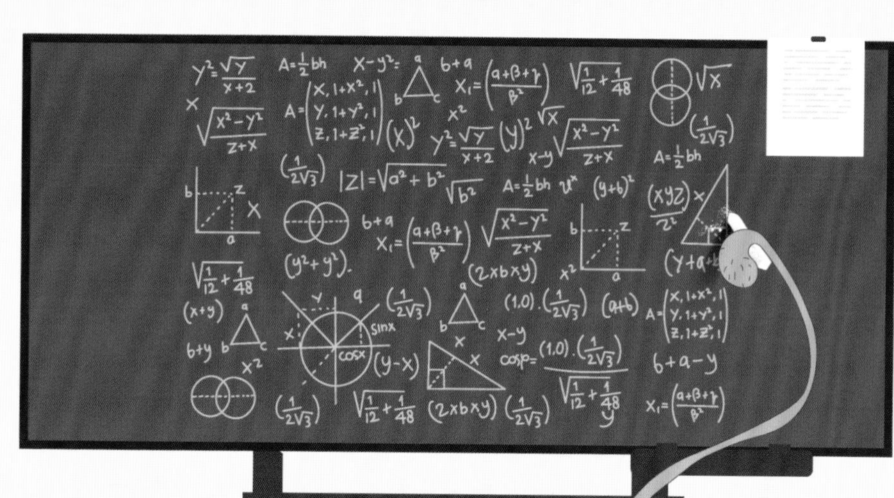

$y^2 = \frac{\sqrt{y}}{x+2}$
$A = \frac{1}{2}bh$
$X_1 = \left(\frac{a+\beta+\gamma}{\beta^2}\right)$
$\sqrt{\frac{1}{12}+\frac{1}{48}}$
$\sqrt{x}$
$\sqrt{\frac{x^2-y^2}{z+x}}$
$\left(\frac{1}{2\sqrt{3}}\right)$
$|Z| = \sqrt{a^2+b^2}$
$\sqrt{b^2}$
$(y+b)^2$
$\frac{(xyz)}{z^2}$
(y^2+y^2)
$(2xbxy)$
$(x+y)$
$(1.0).\left(\frac{1}{2\sqrt{3}}\right)$
$(a+b)$
sinx
cosx
$(y-x)$
$x-y$
$b+a-y$

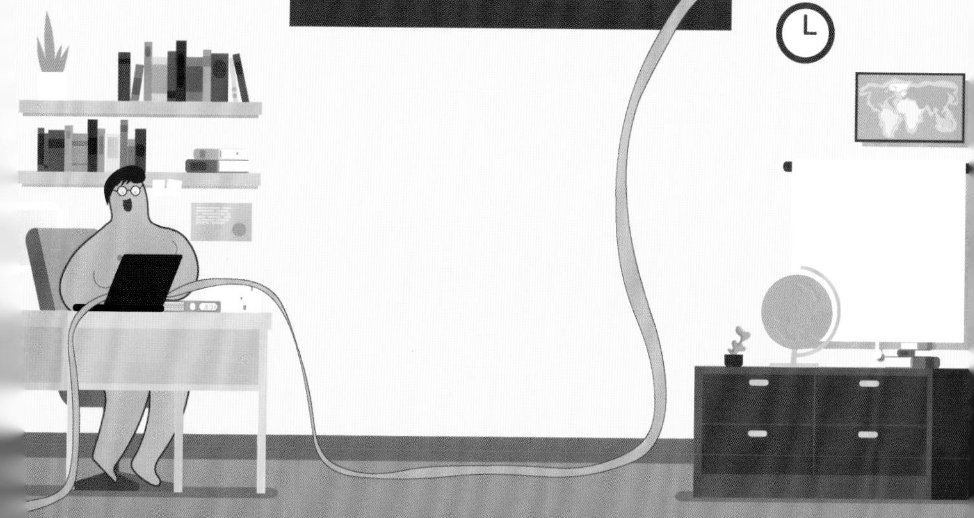

GLACIER BALLS

KITE BALLS

RESCUE CUSHION BALLS

BUSKING BALLS

CURLING BALLS

BUNGEE JUMPING BALLS

CAT SCRATCHER BALLS

CROQUET BALLS

DJ BALLS

DON'T DROP THE SOAP BALLS

FLY SWATTER BALLS

FOOTSTOOL BALLS

FREE RIDE BALLS

GENTLEMAN BALLS
P

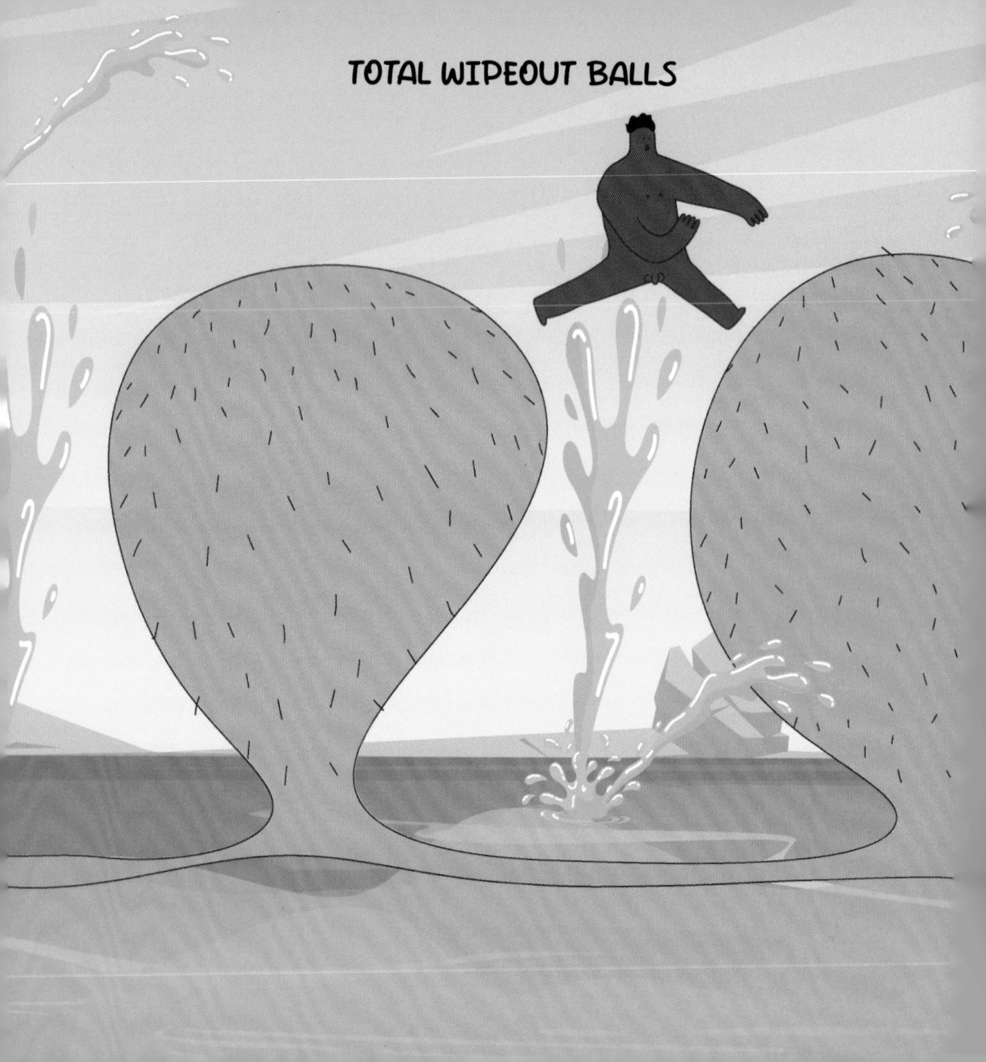
TOTAL WIPEOUT BALLS

ICE FISHING BALLS

KNEE CUSHION BALLS

GRAND OPENING BALLS

INFLATABLE CHAIR BALLS

LASSO BALLS

LIMBO BALLS

NUNCHUCK BALLS

MOP BALLS

DRAW BRIDGE BALLS

ZORB BALLS

NINTH PLANET BALLS

NEW YEARS EVE BALLS
2024

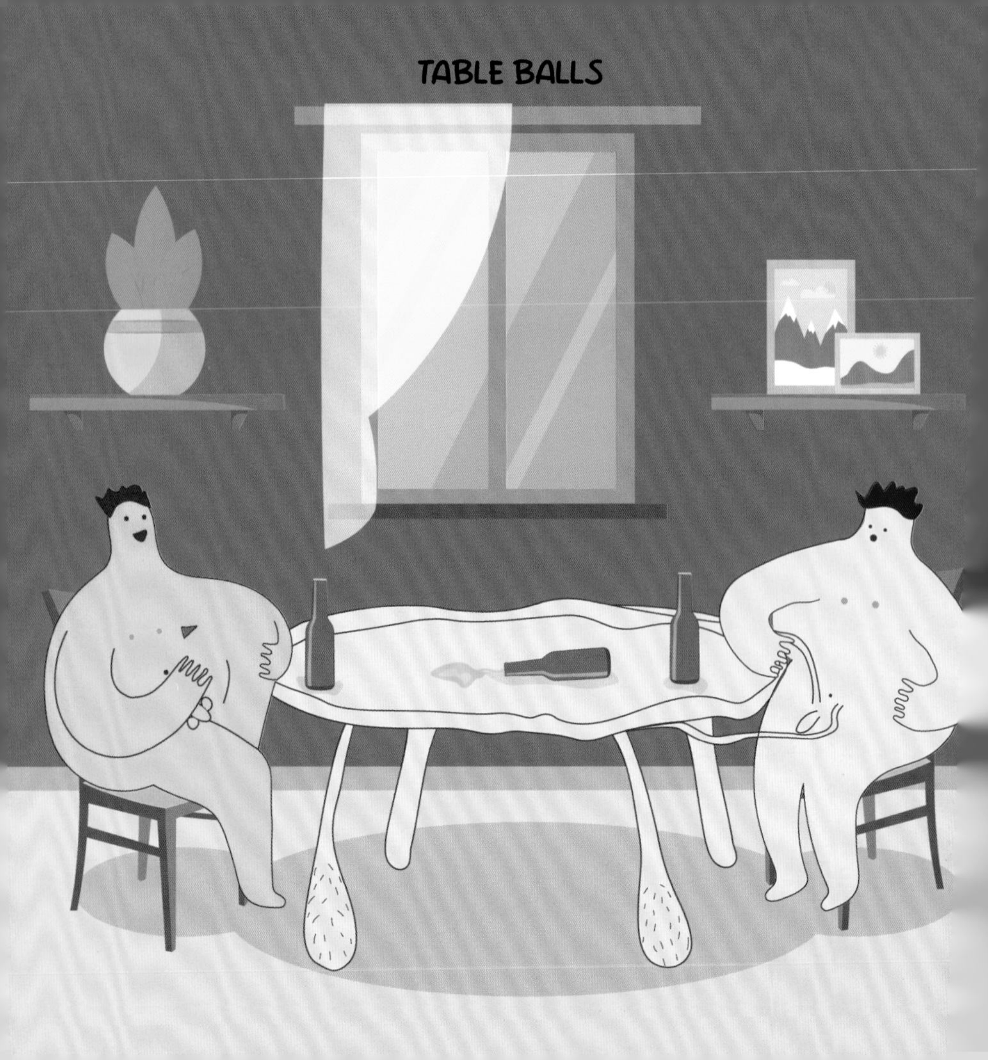
TABLE BALLS

SAIL BOAT BALLS

LOOTING BALLS

TREE SURGEON BALLS

GIFT WRAP BALLS

HAPPY BIRTHDAY!

PUNCHING BAG BALLS

PROPOSAL BALLS

PUNCTURED TYRE BALLS

SOCIAL DISTANCING BALLS

2m

2m

FINISH LINE BALLS
FINISH

SURF BALLS

VAULT GYMNASTICS BALLS

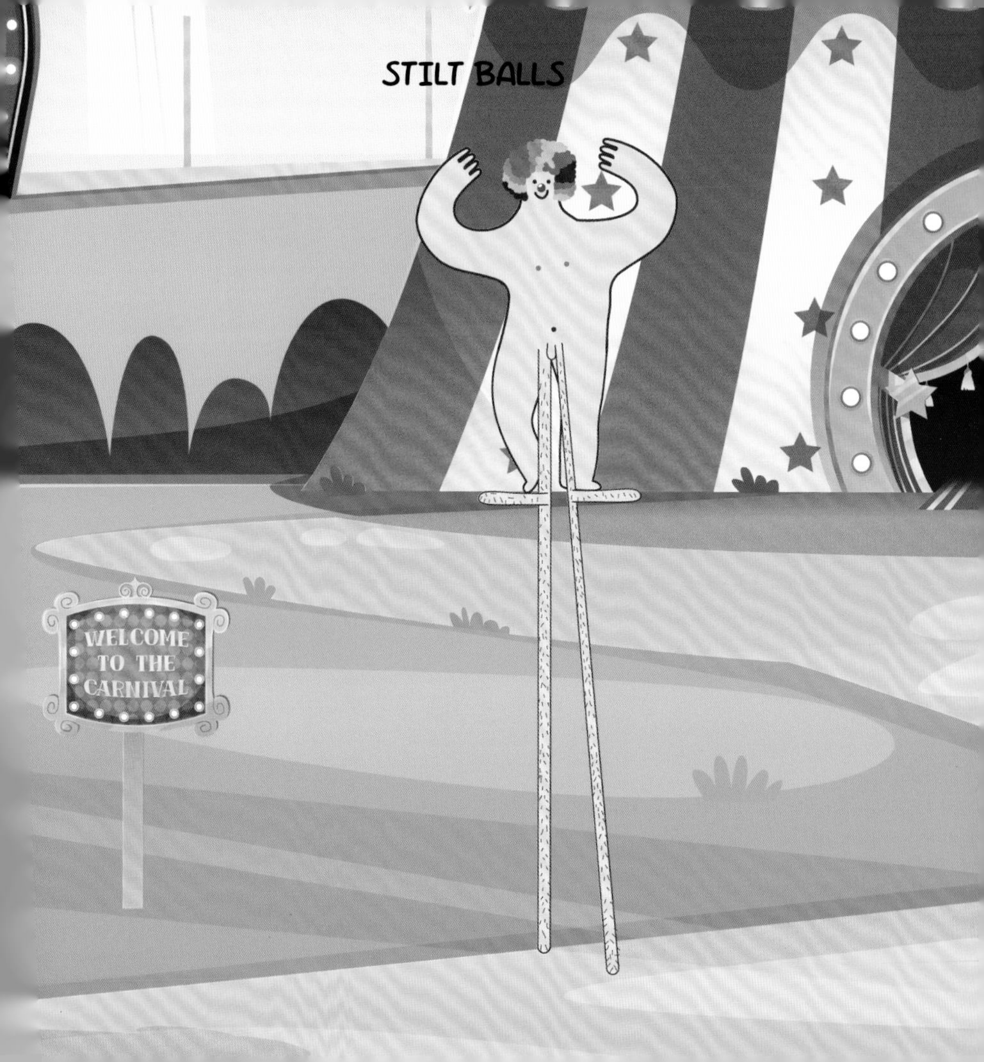
STILT BALLS
WELCOME
TO THE
CARNIVAL

ROOF RACK BALLS

SUPERKING MATTRESS BALLS
Z Z Z

TRAVEL PILLOW BALLS

SKY SCRAPER WINDOW CLEANING BALLS

SUBMARINE BALLS

STEP LADDER BALLS

SWING BALLS

SPEED BUMP BALLS
10
PLEASE
SLOW
DOWN

WATER SKIING BALLS

NOISY NEIGHBOR BALLS

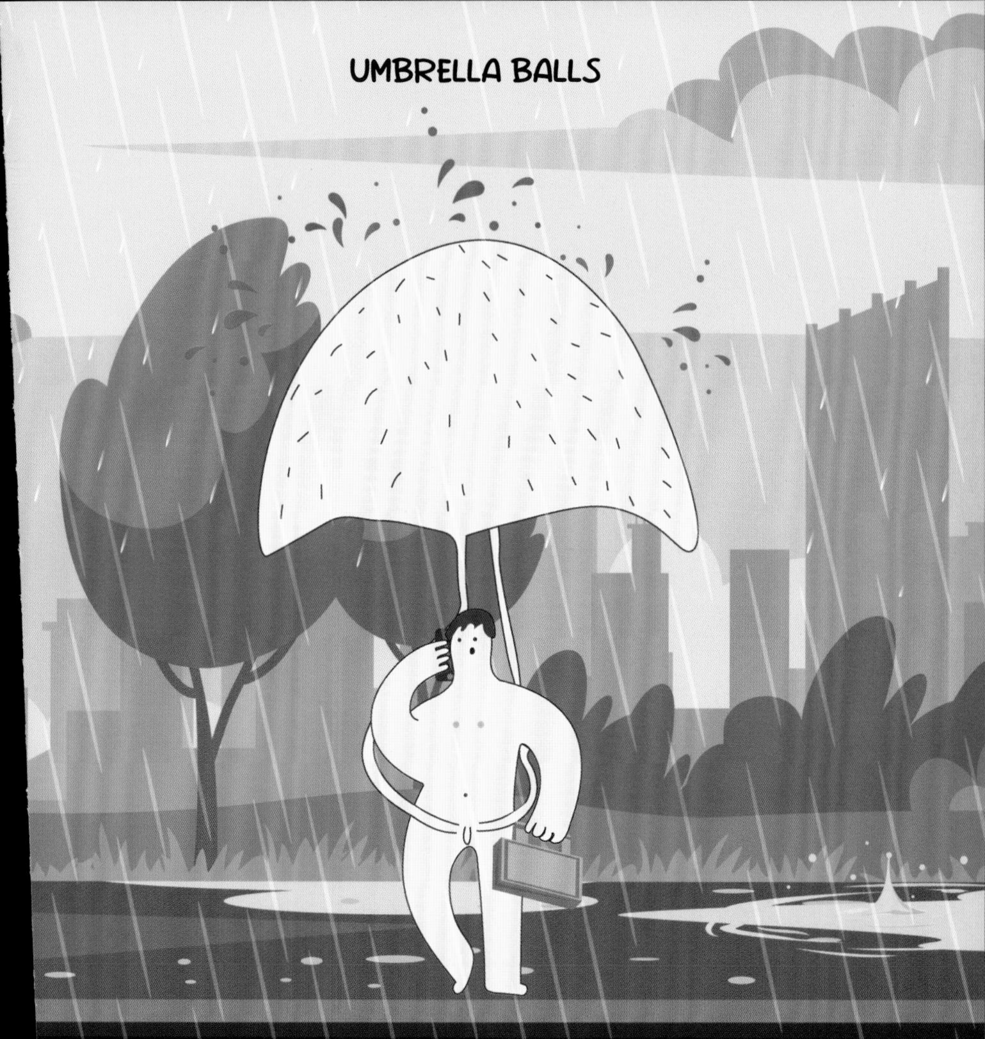
UMBRELLA BALLS

WRECKING BALL BALLS

WELL BALLS

MOUNT RUSHMORE BALLS

WORKING FROM HOME BALLS

TESTING THE WATER BALLS

WALK THE PLANK BALLS

STAGE BALLS

ANCHOR BALLS

AIRBAG BALLS

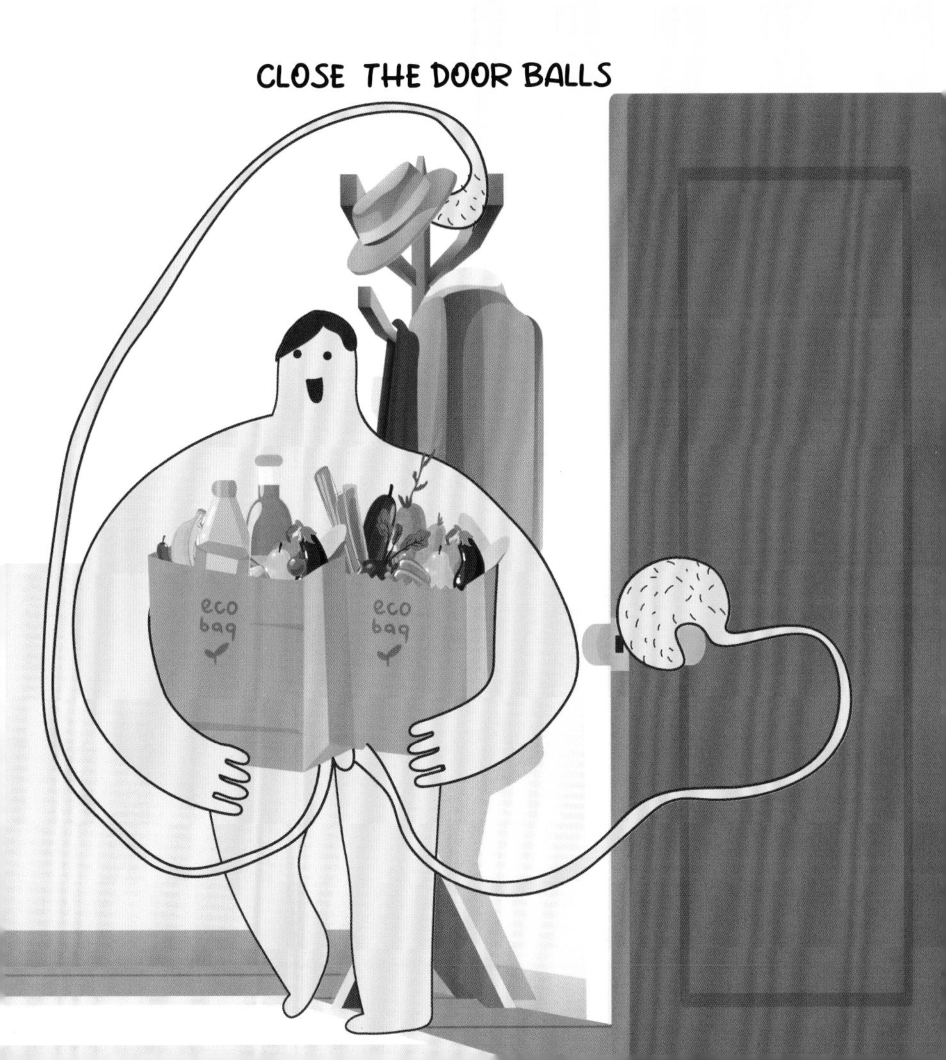
CLOSE THE DOOR BALLS
eco
bag
eco
bag

DOUBLE DUTCH BALLS

WEDDING BALLS

CHRISTMAS TREE BALLS

BATTERING RAM BALLS

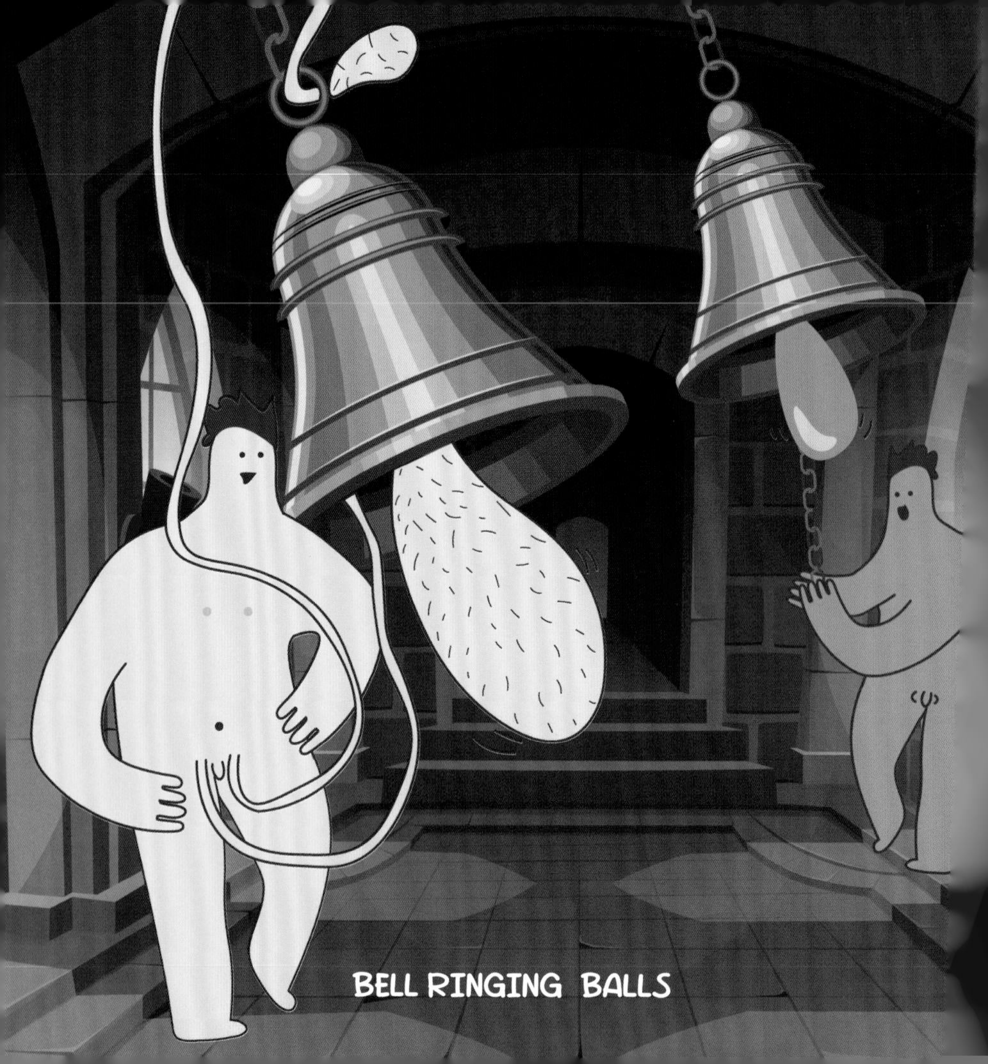
BELL RINGING BALLS

DINOSAUR EXTINCTION BALLS

PIER BALLS

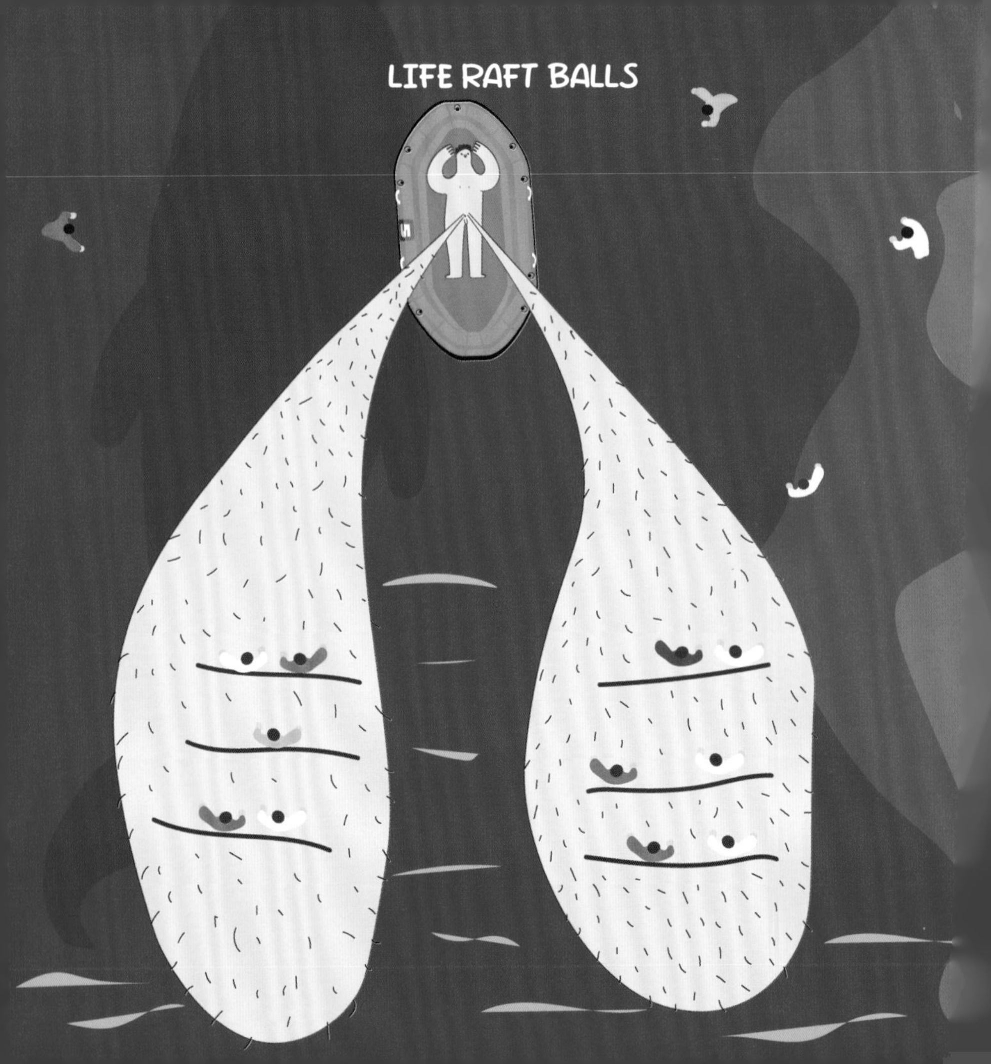
LIFE RAFT BALLS

SPACE HOPPER BALLS

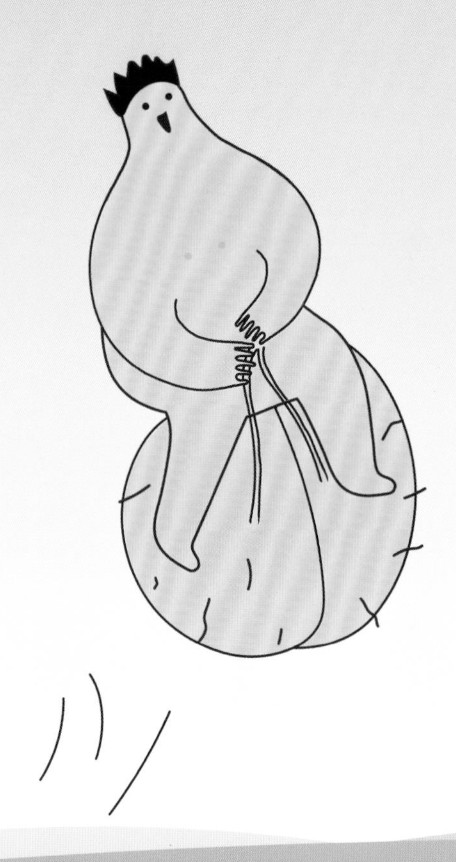

WRESTLING BALLS

TOW TRUCK BALLS

OVEN GLOVE BALLS
160°

MUMMIFICATION BALLS

GATE BALLS

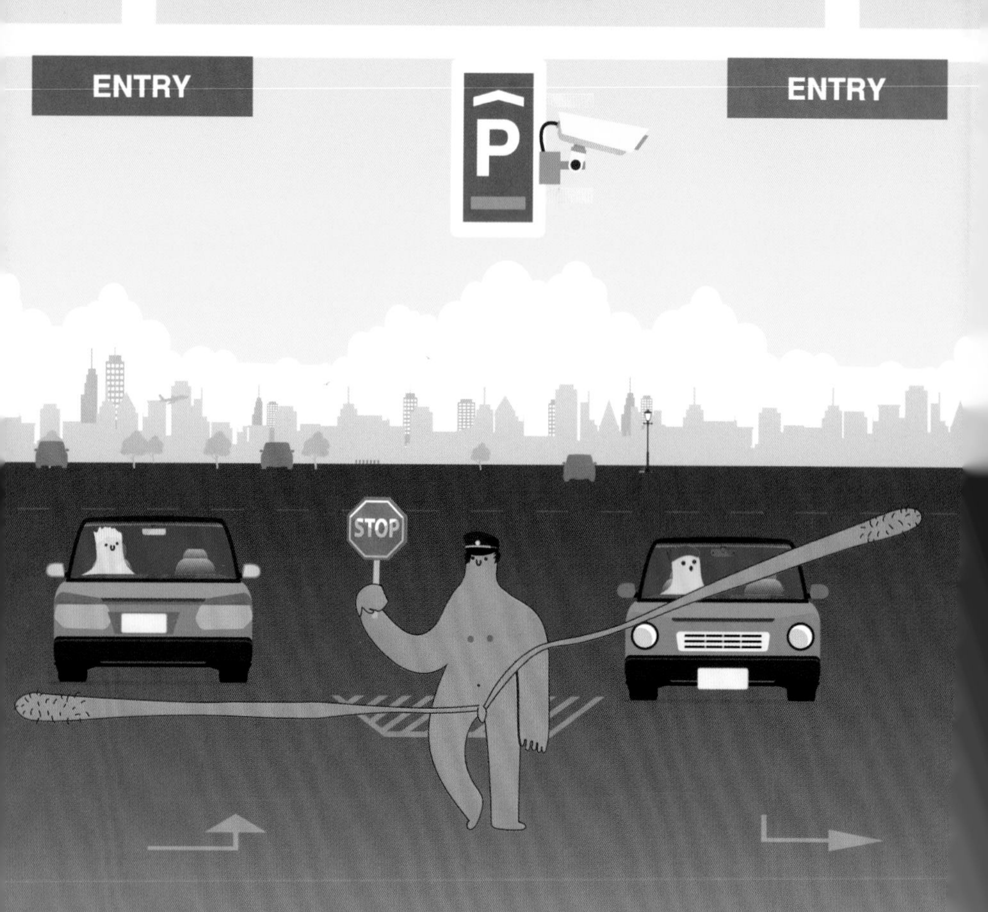

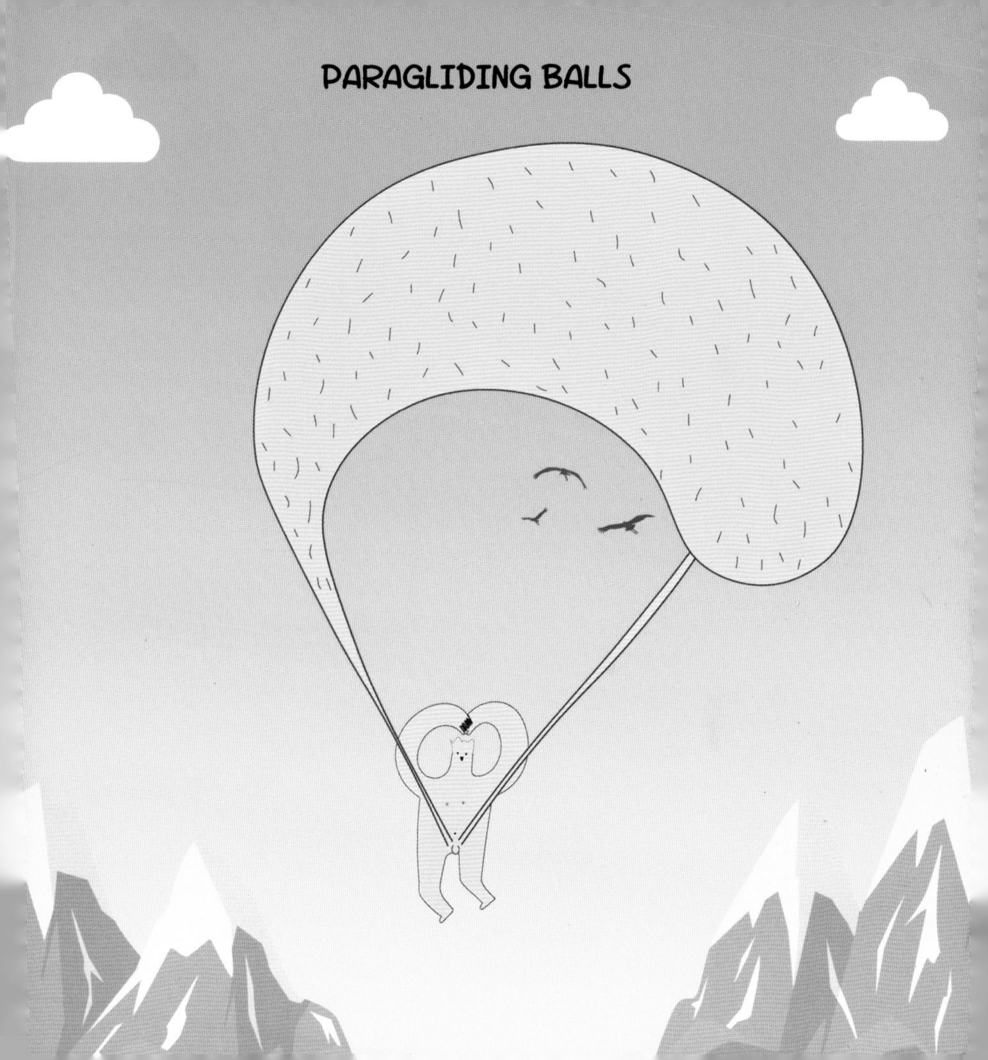
PARAGLIDING BALLS

HOT AIR BALLOON BALLS